AUSTRALIA

First published in Canada by Whitecap Books
351 Lynn Avenue, North Vancouver, British Columbia, V7J 2C4

First published in 2000
Reprinted 2007
Text, maps and illustrations copyright © Random House Australia Pty Ltd,
2000

ISBN 978-1-55285-154-8
ISBN 1-55285-154-0

Children's Publisher: Linsay Knight
Series Editor: Marie-Louise Taylor
Managing Editor: Ariana Klepac
Editor: Selena Quintrell
Art Director: Mark Thacker
Design concept: Stan Lamond
Maps: Cartodraft (Australia) Pty Ltd and Ivan Finnegan Design
Cartographic Co-ordinator: James Mills-Hicks
Production Manager: Linda Watchorn
Publishing Co-ordinator: Pia Gerard

Illustrators: Garry Fleming, pages 17 (below), 28, 30–31, 52–53; Beau
Golden, page 58; Kim Graham, pages 33, 51; David Kirshner, pages 6–7,
33 (above), 42–43, 49 (left); Frank Knight, pages 17 (above), 49 (right);
Iain McKellar, pages 36–37, 56–57; Kevin Stead, page 55; Spike
Wademan, pages 18–19
Educational Consultant: Pamela Hook
Researcher: Peter Barker
Indexer: Bronwyn Sweeney

Film separation by Pica Colour Separation Overseas Pte Ltd, Singapore
Printed in Hong Kong by Sing Cheong Printing Co. Ltd

When you see a word in **bold** type, you'll find its meaning
in the Glossary at the back of the book.

AUSTRALIA

Written by **Margaret McPhee**

whitecap

CONTENTS

CONTENTS

Isolated and unique

Australia has been an island, far away from other lands, for many millions of years. In that long time its animals and plants have slowly changed to become different from those in other parts of the world.

ANCIENT LAND

The rocks that make up the surface of Australia are some of the most ancient on Earth. This is because there have been very few earthquakes or volcanoes to change the land and push up new mountains. Over the ages, old mountains have been worn down by water and wind, and Australia is now the flattest country in the world. The oldest parts of Australia are the vast deserts of the centre and west. The youngest part is the mountainous eastern edge.

LOOK AGAIN!

The frill pops open automatically when the lizard widens its jaws to hiss.

To protect itself from attack, the frilled lizard can spread open an umbrella-like flap of skin, making it look larger, frightening and maybe too spiky to eat!

Putting Australia on the map

Australia is the smallest continent in the world and, because it is surrounded by water, it is also the world's largest inhabited island.

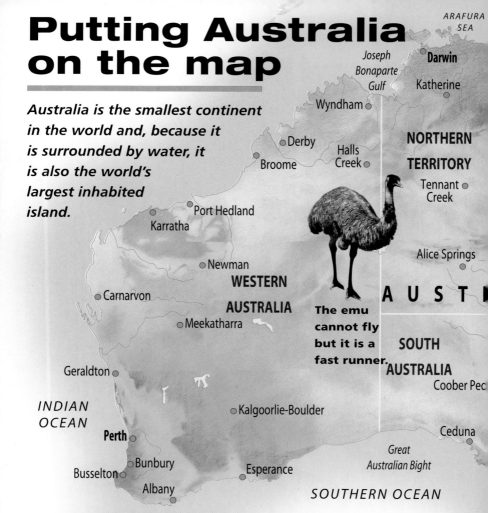

ARAFURA SEA

Joseph Bonaparte Gulf

Darwin

Katherine

Wyndham

Derby

Broome

Halls Creek

NORTHERN TERRITORY

Tennant Creek

Port Hedland

Karratha

Alice Springs

Newman

WESTERN AUSTRALIA

Meekatharra

The emu cannot fly but it is a fast runner.

A U S T

Carnarvon

SOUTH AUSTRALIA

Geraldton

Coober Pec

INDIAN OCEAN

Kalgoorlie-Boulder

Ceduna

Perth

Great Australian Bight

Bunbury

Busselton

Esperance

Albany

SOUTHERN OCEAN

AUSTRALIA DOWN UNDER

Australia is in the southern **hemisphere** of the world. Its seasons are the opposite to those in the northern hemisphere. When it is summer in Australia, it is winter in Europe, China and North America. Australia is the only country that is also a continent. It is made up of six states and two territories. It has tropical rainforests and coral reefs in the north, deserts of red sand in the centre and mountains, forests and fertile plains across most of the south.

Wessel Is

Torres Strait

Gulf of Carpentaria

A roaring waterfall, swollen with summer rain, in Kakadu National Park.

Cairns

Townsville

Mount Isa

Mackay

QUEENSLAND

Rockhampton
Gladstone

Barcaldine

L I A

Maryborough   Fraser I.
Noosa Heads

Charleville

Toowoomba   **Brisbane**

lake Eyre

Wombats dig huge burrows with their powerful legs and shovel-like claws.

Ballina
Grafton
Coffs Harbour

Bourke

Tamworth

Port Macquarie

Broken Hill

Dubbo

Port Augusta
Port Pirie

NEW SOUTH

Orange   Newcastle

valla

Gawler
Adelaide

WALES

Bathurst
Wollongong

Sydney

ort
incoln

Wagga Wagga

Canberra

Murray Bridge

A.C.T.

angaroo l.

Echuca

Mount Kosciuszko

Wangaratta

VICTORIA

Ballarat
Geelong

Melbourne

Mount Gambier

Warrnambool

Fact file

- **Highest point is Mount Kosciuszko, 2,228 metres (7,240 feet), New South Wales**

- **Lowest point is Lake Eyre, South Australia, 15 metres (45 feet) lower than the sea**

Bass Strait   Furneaux
Flinders I.   Group

Burnie   Devonport
Launceston

TASMANIA

Hobart
Bruny I.

9

First Australians

*About 60,000 years ago the **ancestors** of the Aboriginal people began a great voyage south from Asia. Crossing from island to island, they reached the northern shores of Australia, then spread across the land.*

ANCIENT CULTURES

Like the peoples of Europe, Aboriginal people developed into many groups with different languages and different ways. All groups had stories about how great spirit-beings made the land, animals and plants and gave the people laws and ceremonies. They believe that certain landforms, such as a waterhole, or a hill or rock with a special shape, are places where the spirit-beings rested, fought or found food.

Music and dance are an important way of passing on stories about the land and its creatures. A big gathering like this is called a corroboree.

LOOK AGAIN!

The body paint is made from clay and coloured rocks crushed into powder.

Above: Aboriginal hunters kill only what is needed for food. This hunter may spear a wallaby or use his boomerang (throwing stick) to bring down a duck. Women and children collect roots, seeds and fruits. Left: A performer decorated and ready to dance.

The Australian Capital Territory

The Australian Capital Territory is a special area chosen in 1908 for Australia's capital city, Canberra.

CANBERRA

The designers of Canberra won a world-wide competition. Before the city was built the land was hills and sheep fields. Parks and gardens now run down to an artificial lake. The country's important buildings are grouped either side of the water in an area called the Parliamentary Triangle. Hills covered with gum trees and native flowers rise up on the edge of the city.

Parliament House is built into the top of a hill. The roof is grassed over and you can walk on it while politicians work below. The flag flying from the huge flagpole is as big as a double-decker bus.

LOOK AGAIN!

The Australian Capital Territory is completely surrounded by New South Wales.

Fact file

Area: 2359 square kilometres (911 square miles)

Capital: Canberra

Population: 324,000

Floral emblem: Royal bluebell

These huge antennae at the Tidbinbilla Space Tracking Station pick up signals from spacecraft exploring the outer parts of our Solar System.

NEW SOUTH

WALES

Hall

Ginninderra

Belconnen

Lake Burley Griffin

Braddon

● **Canberra**

South Canberra

Fyshwick

Weston Creek

Woden Valley

Tuggeranong

Murrumbidgee

Namadgi National Park

Tharwa

Royalla

rin Dam

Williamsdale

AUSTRALIAN

CAPITAL

TERRITORY

NEW SOUTH

WALES

Thousands of kangaroos live in the hills in the southern part of the Australian Capital Territory.

More than half the Australian Capital Territory is bush. In spring it is bright with wildflowers, such as these nectar-filled banksia blooms.

The people of Australia

People from all over the world have come to Australia to settle. Today they are learning to live together in harmony in a multicultural society.

PEOPLE FROM EVERYWHERE

The first **immigrants** to this land were the Aborigines who moved south from Asia many thousands of years ago. The first Europeans to settle were convicts transported from England in 1788. When gold was discovered in 1851, treasure seekers from Europe, America and China rushed to find their fortune. After World War II ended in 1945, immigrants came from Europe. More recently, people have migrated from all over the world to start a new life.

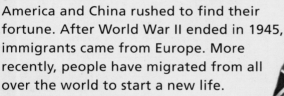

Aboriginal culture is rich in traditions of stories, art, craft, music, dance and drama.

The Australian flag is a symbol for all Australians. The Southern Cross on the flag is seen in Australian skies.

A multicultural society is one where people of many races and cultures live together.

Most Australians live along the coast, in cities and towns, but many prefer the quiet of the country.

New South Wales

New South Wales covers about one-tenth of Australia. It has long sandy beaches, high mountains and wide plains.

THE FIRST STATE

New South Wales was the first place in Australia where Europeans came to live. Today it has the country's largest population and its largest city, Sydney. Most people in New South Wales live along the coast. West of the Great Dividing Range are plains where farmers grow crops and raise sheep and cattle. Further west, where there is little rainfall, the plains become desert.

QUEENSLAN

Tibooburra

SOUTH AUSTRALIA

Darling

Broken Hill

NEW SOU

Mildura

About 30,000 years ago these dry sands at Lake Mungo, north of Mildura, were the green banks of a lake.

Speeding past the Opera House, a ferry carries passengers across Sydney Harbour.

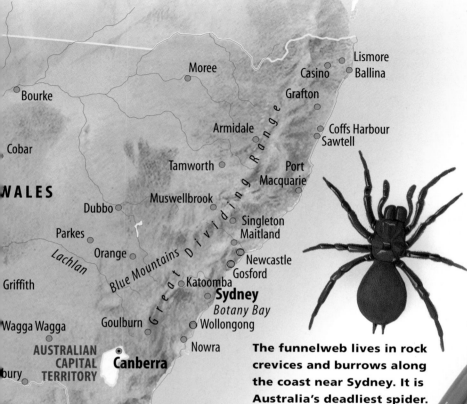

Moree
Bourke
Casino • Lismore
Ballina
Grafton
Cobar
Armidale
Great Dividing Range
Coffs Harbour
Sawtell
WALES
Tamworth
Port
Macquarie
Muswellbrook
Dubbo
Singleton
Maitland
Parkes
Orange
Newcastle
Lachlan
Gosford
Blue Mountains
Griffith
Katoomba
Sydney
Botany Bay
Wagga Wagga
Goulburn
Wollongong
AUSTRALIAN
Nowra
CAPITAL
bury
TERRITORY
Canberra
VICTORIA
Tasman Sea
Eden

The funnelweb lives in rock crevices and burrows along the coast near Sydney. It is Australia's deadliest spider.

Fact file

Area: 801,428 square kilometres (309,432 square miles)
Capital: Sydney
Population: 6,875,700
Floral emblem: Waratah

The green and golden bell frog lives on rushes beside streams, swamps and lagoons. Non-native fish eat its tadpoles, and it is now rare. Some of these frogs live safely in an old quarry beside Sydney Olympic Park.

LOOK AGAIN!

Sailors are taking down the top sails to stop them from being torn in the storm.

18

Terra Australis

'Terra Australis' *means 'Southern Land'. Europeans used this name for the continent they believed must exist in the south to balance the lands of the north.*

VOYAGE TO THE UNKNOWN

In the 1600s Dutch sailors on their way to Java (Indonesia) saw Australia's western coast. They called it 'New Holland'. In 1770 English **navigator** James Cook explored the eastern coast of Australia. He called the land 'New South Wales', because it reminded him of South Wales in the United Kingdom. The First Fleet, carrying the first Europeans to live in Australia, arrived from England in 1788. Those on board were mostly **convicts**. Guarded by **marines**, they built a small town at Sydney Cove, between where the Harbour Bridge and the Opera House now stand.

Officers and officials travelled in cabins. Convicts were crammed behind bars in the bottom of the ship and allowed on deck for fresh air only once a day. Disease spread quickly in the filthy conditions and many convicts died at sea.

Those on board the First Fleet took eight months to sail to Australia and had to wait more than two years for news from Europe. Today the same journey takes less than 24 hours and news takes less than a second.

Living on the edge

Although Australia is a vast country, most people live along its edges. They share the coast with passing whales, playful dolphins and sometimes even roaming sharks.

Bondi Beach is a long curve of golden sand not far from the centre of Sydney. It is Australia's most famous beach.

Early every summer, kite flyers from all over Australia gather at Bondi for the Festival of the Winds. Their colourful kites in all sorts of fantastic shapes and sizes fill the sky, soaring and swooping above the waves.

AT THE BEACH

Australia's largest cities are all close to beaches. In summer the beaches are like huge free fun parks with people swimming, riding surfboards, playing in the sand or jogging along the water's edge. Lifesavers set up flags to show the safest place to swim. The beaches where most people swim have shark nets offshore, so sharks and swimmers rarely meet. You are far more likely to see whales making their long winter trip between feeding grounds in the cold south and the warmer waters of northern Australia.

LOOK AGAIN!

Lifesavers are easy to see in their red and yellow caps. Their flags are red and yellow too.

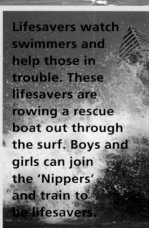

Lifesavers watch swimmers and help those in trouble. These lifesavers are rowing a rescue boat out through the surf. Boys and girls can join the 'Nippers' and train to be lifesavers.

Victoria

This state was named after Queen Victoria of England. Victorians see their state as being 'on the move' because it is fast becoming a world famous city for business and tourism.

THE GARDEN STATE

Victoria is also called 'The Garden State' because much of the country is natural bushland and its rich soils can grow a variety of crops. Fertile farming land rolls down to the sea and here herds of dairy cattle feed contentedly and farmers grow crops. Years ago paddle steamers carried wheat and wool from inland farms south along the mighty Murray River. Today the river irrigates farms of rice, fruit and wheat. Tourists marvel at the spectacular rock formations carved out by the ocean along the southern coastline.

LOOK AGAIN!

The Murray River forms the northern border of Victoria. Can you trace its path?

SOUTH AUSTRALIA

Mildura

Robinvale

Ouyen

Warracknabeal

Nhill

Horsham

Mt William

Hamilton

Portland

Warnambool

Cape Nelson

Melbourne trams carry people all over the city. Sometimes trams are specially painted to celebrate events.

Shearing is a busy time for sheep farmers in Victoria. The fleece is shorn from the sheep with special clippers that trim fast but don't injure the animal. Shearers are very proud of the number of sheep they can shear in a day.

Fact file

Area: 227,600 square kilometres (87,877 square miles)
Capital: Melbourne
Population: 5,188,100
Floral emblem: Pink heath

Kookaburras are famous for their call, which resembles loud raucous laughter.

NEW SOUTH WALES

Swan Hill
Kerang
Murray
Echuca
Shepparton
Wangaratta
Wodonga

Bendigo

VICTORIA

Mt Hotham ▲

Great Dividing Range

Snowy Mountains

Ballarat
Sunbury
Melbourne
Melton
Geelong
Torquay
Port Phillip Bay
Rye
Colac
Phillip Island
Moe
Wonthaggi
Morwell
Sale
Bairnsdale
Orbost
Lakes Entrance
Ninety Mile Beach

Cape Howe

TASMAN SEA

Cape Otway

Wilsons Promontory

Bass Strait

Australians at play

Australians like to play all kinds of sport. Many champion swimmers, tennis players, runners, rowers and cricketers come from Australia.

Surging back to shore on a huge wave. Great skill is needed to balance on the board and control its direction. Surfboard riders must also be strong swimmers.

LOOK AGAIN!

Both cricket players and bike riders wear helmets to protect their heads.

FUN IN THE OPEN

There is lots of space and the weather is warm and dry, so people can play sport and have fun outdoors all year. Long summers mean watersports are a favourite. There are outdoor pools in the suburbs and country towns, and for most Australians, the beach is not far away. Cricket, tennis and basketball are also popular in summer. In winter Australians play four types of football, including soccer. Some people play hockey. Some even ski down the snowy slopes of the Australian Alps.

Young and old cycle for fun and for fitness. Many parks have special tracks for bicycles.

Cricketers wear white clothes and special equipment when playing for school or for a club. Cricket is a popular sport for both girls and boys.

Australian Rules Football players leaping for the ball. This type of football was invented in Victoria and is now played in most parts of the country.

Unique Australians

A marsupial is a mammal which has a pouch for its young. Most of the world's marsupials are found only in Australia. Kangaroos, possums, wombats and koalas are all marsupials.

AMONG THE GUM TREES

Gum trees (eucalypts) developed in Australia. Tall gum tree forests like this grow on moist mountain slopes. Tree ferns and flowering bushes grow near the ground. Wallabies and kangaroos shelter here during the day, and at dusk move off to grasslands to graze. Echidnas, looking for ants, shuffle through leaves on the forest floor. In the leafy treetops, flocks of noisy parrots search for blossoms and seeds. Possums come out at night, leaping fearlessly from branch to branch. Small bats emerge from hollows to hunt insects.

Koalas eat only gum leaves. They get all the moisture they need from the leaves, and normally do not need to drink. Although there are more than 500 different kinds of eucalypt tree, there are only about thirty that koalas eat. During the day koalas sleep high in the trees in the forks of branches.

LOOK
AGAIN!
The brushtail possum
has large eyes to
see better at night,
when it feeds.

The brushtail possum makes a nest
in a hollow branch. When the
young grows too big for the
pouch, it rides on its mother's
back. This possum is eating gum
leaves. Brushtail possums also eat
fruit, flowers and even tree bark.

The rainbow lorikeet has
tiny brushes on its tongue
to wipe nectar and pollen
from blossoms. The birds
fly in groups to find food.
Then they clamber over the
outer branches, chattering
non-stop as they feed.

Queensland

In 1859, Queen Victoria, the ruler of England at the time requested that this new colony be named after her. Today Queensland has been nicknamed 'The Sunshine State' and all who live and visit there enjoy the outdoor life.

THE SUNSHINE STATE

Queensland stretches north towards the Equator. In the north, steamy rainforests clothe the slopes of the Great Dividing Range that runs the length of the east coast. Along the coastal plain, sugar cane, bananas and pineapples grow in the rich soil. At harvest time, cane farmers set fire to their fields to burn the leaves so the stalks can be easily cut. West of the mountains the climate is drier, and cattle and sheep are raised. Many rivers flow into the Gulf of Carpentaria and these abound in saltwater crocodiles.

Cane toads were brought to Australia to eat certain beetles that were damaging the sugar cane. These toads have now become a real pest. Special glands in their skin produce poison that can kill predators.

NORTHERN TERRITORY

To attract a female, the male satin bower bird decorates a special leafy room (called a bower) with bright objects.

Torres Strait

Bamaga

Cape York

Cape York Peninsula

Gulf of Carpentaria

Cooktown

Cairns

Mornington I.

Bentinck I.

Karumba

Georgetown

VH-MSU

The Royal Flying Doctor Service visits patients in the outback.

Fact file

Area: 1,727,200 square kilometres (666,875 square miles)
Capital: Brisbane
Population: 4,162,000
Floral emblem: Cooktown orchid

Great Barrier Reef

Townsville

The Storey Bridge spans the Brisbane River.

Mount Isa

Great Dividing Range

Mackay

Sarina

QUEENSLAND

Barcaldine

Emerald

Rockhampton

Gladstone

Hervey Bay

Diamantina

Cooper

Windorah

Charleville

Darling Downs

Maryborough

Fraser I.

Noosa Heads

Nambour

OUTH TRALIA

Sturt Desert

Balonne

Toowoomba

Ipswich

Brisbane

NEW SOUTH

WALES

The Great Barrier Reef

The Great Barrier Reef is a long band of about 3,000 separate coral reefs. It is the largest structure in the world made by living creatures.

TEEMING WONDERLAND

Coral reefs are built up by tiny sea animals called coral **polyps**. Each polyp produces a material like cement to make a hard outside skeleton. When it dies, a new polyp builds on the remains, and so the reef slowly grows. Inside its 'house', the polyp is like a soft tube. It feeds at night by pushing out a ring of waving tentacles to sweep in passing food particles. Creatures of all colours, shapes and sizes live and feed in the caves and passageways of the reef and in the warm, clear waters around it.

LOOK AGAIN!

The colours of the corals come from living polyps. Dead coral is white.

A huge manta ray glides near the surface. The loggerhead turtle is clumsy on land, but 'flies' through the water with its paddle-like flippers.

The best way to see underwater creatures is by snorkelling or diving, or through the floor of a glass-bottomed boat. Touching or standing on the reef damages living coral.

The crown-of-thorns starfish is covered with long, poisonous spines. It feeds on live coral polyps. Sometimes these starfish appear in large numbers and kill parts of the Great Barrier Reef.

Daintree wonderland

Daintree National Park is one of the few places in the world where rainforest meets white sandy beaches and coral reef.

CROWDED FOREST

More types of plants and animals are found in this rugged rainforest than anywhere else in Australia. Some plants have not changed since the dinosaurs lived, and grow nowhere else on Earth. Tall trees spread their leafy branches to get as much sunlight as possible. Little light reaches through to the damp forest floor where brush-turkeys and cassowaries scratch in the rotting leaves for snails, scurrying beetles, fungi and fallen fruits.

Like its relative the emu, the cassowary cannot fly. When running through the forest it lowers its head and uses the bony bump on top (called a casque) to push aside vines, ferns and branches.

This green tree frog leaps to snare an insect with a flick of its sticky tongue, then flips the catch to the back of its mouth.

A chain of tiny green tree ants drag leaves together. Using sticky silk squeezed from their larvae (young), these ants weave living leaves into a nest as big as a football.

LOOK AGAIN!
The frog needs wide jaws because it swallows its food whole. It only eats what will fit through.

Fact file

Area: 2,525,500 square kilometres (975,101 square miles)
Capital: Perth
Population: 2,094,500
Floral emblem: Kangaroo paw

Joseph
Cape Londonderry · Bonaparte
Gulf

Wyndham
K i m b e r l e y
P l a t e a u
Lake
Argyle
Derby
Broome
Fitzroy Crossing
Halls Creek

Great Sandy
Desert

TIMOR SEA

Barrow I.
Port Hedland
North West
Cape
Karratha

P i l b a r a

H a m e r s l e y   R a n g e

Lake
Mackay

Ashburton
Newman

Shark
Bay
Carnarvon
▲ Mt Augustus

Murchison

Meekatharra

Lake
Carnegie

WESTERN

AUSTRALIA

Geraldton

Lake
Barlee

Lake
Moore

INDIAN
OCEAN

Kalgoorlie-Boulder

Perth
Fremantle
Rockingham
Bunbury
Busselton

Nulla

Eucla

Cape Leeuwin
Point d'Entrecastax
Esperance

Albany

Cape Pasley

Great
Australian Bight

34

SOUTHERN OCEAN

Budgerigars are small parrots. After winter rains, large flocks search for grass seeds on inland plains.

Wheat is grown in the south west of the state where the summers are long and hot and the rain falls in winter.

Western Australia

When each Australian region became a new state, there were often arguments about its new name. Western Australia was almost called 'Hesperia' meaning 'land looking west'.

NORTHERN TERRITORY

THE LARGEST STATE

Western Australia is the largest state with great stony deserts at its centre. Western Australia has its own beautiful coral reef off the north west coast and its own meteor crater in the rugged Kimberley district, west of Wyndham. Dinosaur footprints can be seen near Broome. The Nullarbor Plain is a dry riverless flat strip of desert which hugs the southern coastline, east of Esperance. 'Nullarbor' means 'no trees'. The state has great mineral wealth and iron ore, uranium, oil and gold are mined. Most people live near the capital, Perth.

SOUTH AUSTRALIA

Plain

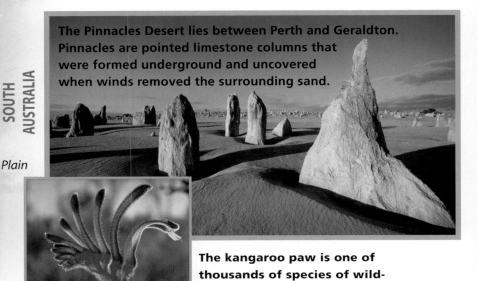

The Pinnacles Desert lies between Perth and Geraldton. Pinnacles are pointed limestone columns that were formed underground and uncovered when winds removed the surrounding sand.

The kangaroo paw is one of thousands of species of wild-flowers that grow in this state.

Bushfire!

Australia is the driest continent. More fires sweep across its surface than any other land. Buildings and crops are destroyed and sometimes animals and people die.

DESIGNED TO BURN

Australian plants have developed ways of living with bushfire. In the eucalypt forest, flames leap through the treetops, quickly burning the **flammable** oil in the leaves and then racing on, leaving the main part of the tree to regrow from leaf buds hidden under the bark. Many plants need bushfire to burst open their hard pods so the seeds can scatter. Some seeds need smoke to **germinate**. After a fire, the forests and grasslands are soon covered with healthy new plants.

Bushfires are started either by lightning strikes or accidentally or deliberately by humans. Strong winds blow burning embers ahead, spreading the flames rapidly through the dry forest. The raging fire roars like a jumbo jet.

Unlike plants, animals have no special ways of living with bushfires. They must flee through the choking smoke, like these kangaroos and cockatoos. Only the fast will survive.

LOOK AGAIN!
The firefighters are wearing special clothing to protect them from the flames.

Mining

Many important metals and precious stones are found in rocks across the vast continent of Australia. Some of the biggest mines in the world are here.

RICHES FROM THE EARTH

Australia sells iron ore, copper, bauxite (used to make aluminium), coal (used to make electricity), gold and silver to other countries. The income earned is important to Australia. Mining can destroy trees, rivers and special places. When the mining is finished, the mining company must carefully replace the earth and replant it with the right trees and flowers. Australia also has precious stones, such as diamonds and opals.

A blast breaks up rock at the Argyle Diamond Mine, Western Australia. The rock is then crushed by a machine so the hard diamonds can be removed.

LOOK AGAIN!

This truck is as high as a single storey house. The driver needs a ladder to reach the cabin.

When the ore (rock rich with metal) is near the surface it can be taken away in layers. This is called open-cut mining.

Huge trucks carry massive loads of ore to crushers. These trucks are too big for public roads. They never leave the mine.

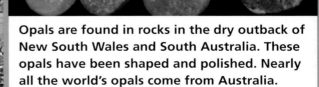

Opals are found in rocks in the dry outback of New South Wales and South Australia. These opals have been shaped and polished. Nearly all the world's opals come from Australia.

Tasmania

This island state was named after Abel Tasman, a Dutch explorer who charted its coastline in 1642. Tasmania has been called 'The Holiday Isle' because there is so much to see and do there.

Cape
Wickho

Currie

King

THE ISLAND STATE

Tasmania has been an island for thousands of years. The large islands in Bass Strait, off the northern coast, are also part of the state. Central Tasmania is a high area of jagged mountains. Farmland covers much of the north—from the air the land looks like a patchwork quilt of browns and greens. The west is mostly rugged wilderness. On the east coast are beaches of white sand. Hobart, the capital, has a beautiful harbour and every year ocean-going yachts race from Sydney to Hobart across stormy Bass Strait.

The Tasmanian devil is a marsupial. It was given its name by early settlers who were frightened by its piercing screams. At night the devil hunts for possums, wallabies and wombats. It also finds and eats dead animals. With its powerful jaws and sharp teeth it eats every part of its prey, even bones.

Cradle Mountain is a beautiful spot to enjoy the snow in winter and to go bushwalking in summer.

Fact file

Area: 68,331 square kilometres (26,383 square miles)
Capital: Hobart
Population: 492,700
Floral emblem: Tasmanian blue gum

BASS STRAIT

ree Hummock I.
Hunter I.

t
t

Stanley
Smithton
Burnie
George Town
Devonport
Scottsdale
Launceston

Flinders I.
Furneaux Group
Cape Barren I.
Clarke I.
Banks Strait

TASMAN SEA

Eddystone Pt.
St Helens

Cradle Mountain
Mt Ossa
Macquarie
Great Lake

Queenstown
Strahan

Macquarie Harbour

TASMANIA

Swansea

Derwent

Oyster Bay

The south west is a wilderness of mountains, rainforests and fast-flowing rivers where kayaking is a popular sport.

SOUTHERN OCEAN

Lake Gordon
Sorell

Hobart

Geeveston
Kingston

Southport
Port Arthur

South Bruny I.
South East Cape

Not far from Hobart are the ruins of a convict prison called Port Arthur.

Monotremes

*Monotremes are a very unusual kind of **mammal**. Unlike other mammals, monotremes lay eggs. The eggs have soft, leathery shells and hatch after about ten days. The mother does not have teats. Instead milk oozes through the skin on her belly to be lapped up by her tiny, hairless young.*

At dusk and dawn the platypus hunts for food. A furrow of skin closes over its eyes and ears when it dives, so it cannot see or hear underwater. Searching with its sensitive bill, the platypus finds insects and small water creatures on the muddy bottom. The catch is stored in cheek pouches to eat later.

LOOK AGAIN!

The platypus' bill is leathery and can bend, it is not hard and bony like a duck's bill.

When the first platypus skin arrived in England, scientists thought that the bill and feet of a duck and the fur of a rabbit had been sewn together to fool people.

LIVING FOSSILS

Fossils show that ancient monotremes were on the Earth at the same time as the dinosaurs. Today there are two kinds of monotreme—the platypus, found only in Australia, and the echidna (spiny anteater), found in Australia and New Guinea. The echidna has a coat of long, sharp, thin spikes and rolls into a prickly ball if attacked. It catches ants and small insects with its long sticky tongue.

The platypus is the world's only venomous mammal. A sharp hollow spur on each back leg of the male is connected to poison glands in the thighs.

South Australia

Australians call South Australia 'The Festival State' and it has much to celebrate. There are festivals in Adelaide, opals in Coober Pedy, wine in the Barossa Valley and big game fishing in Port Lincoln.

THE DRIEST STATE

Much of South Australia is semi-desert and only about one tenth of the land can be farmed. Many of its lakes are dry and covered by a shining layer of salt. South Australia did not begin as a convict settlement. People travelled from England to farm the fertile land in the south east and produce wheat, wool, beef and lamb. Many German people settled in the Barossa Valley, north of Adelaide, where they grew grapes for wine. Today South Australia is famous for wines.

WESTERN AUSTRALIA

A blue-tongued lizard displays its brightly coloured tongue when it is angry or disturbed. It is well adapted to dry conditions.

Harvesting grapes in the Barossa Valley is a busy time for wine makers. Barossa means 'hillside of roses'.

▲ *Mt Woodroffe* *Alberga*

usgrave Ranges

In the opal mining town of Coober Pedy, people live in underground houses to escape the heat.

Oodnadatta

Cooper Creek

SOUTH AUSTRALIA

Lake Eyre North

Coober Pedy

Lake Maurice

LOOK AGAIN!

South Australia is bordered by four states and one territory. Can you name them?

Lake Eyre South

● *Marree*

Lake Frome

Lake Torrens

aralinga

Lake Macfarlane

Lake Gairdner

● *Penong*

● *Ceduna*

Great Australian Bight

● Port Augusta

Whyalla ●

● Port Pirie

SOUTHERN

OCEAN

Spencer Gulf

Murray

● Gawler

Adelaide

Port Lincoln ●

Gulf St Vincent

● Murray Bridge

Fact file

Area: 984,000 square
kilometres (379,925 square
miles)
Capital: Adelaide
Population: 1,581,400
Floral emblem: Sturt's
desert pea

Kangaroo I.

Encounter Bay

Cape Jaffa

Mount Gambier ●

QUEENSLAND

NEW SOUTH WALES

VICTORIA

45

The red centre

Deserts of red sand stretch across the centre of Australia. Plants and animals there have developed many ways to survive the hot days and lack of water.

DESERT LIFE

Desert animals stay in their nests and burrows, or rest under bushes, during the hot day. This means their bodies use up less moisture. They come out to feed when it is cooler. Some animals can go for weeks without drinking by getting all the moisture they need from their food. Insects have hard thick shells to stop them drying out. Plants grow low to the ground to shade their roots and stop water evaporating. Life speeds up when rare rain falls. Seeds quickly germinate, grow, flower and set seed. Many animals **mate** and raise their young before the water disappears.

The dingo is a wild dog. It is related to the wolf. Dingoes hunt alone or in small family groups. They eat anything from kangaroos to insects and even berries.

LOOK AGAIN!
Small creatures are sheltering from the sun in the spinifex clumps.

Grooves in the thorny devil's spiky skin channel even the smallest drop of water from anywhere on its body directly into its mouth. Despite its terrifying appearance, this small lizard is a danger only to ants.

The red kangaroo lives on the dry plains of inland Australia. It lies in shade during the day and feeds at night on grass and leaves. When hopping quickly, a kangaroo takes off from and lands on its back toes. Its strong tail is used for balance.

Deadly creatures

There are more kinds of creatures that can kill you in Australia than on any other continent. Fortunately, most stay well away from people.

The great white shark prefers seals but sometimes attacks people, perhaps by mistake. Its triangular teeth are razor-sharp.

LOOK OUT!

Some of the most dangerous creatures are found at the beach. Sea wasps are jellyfish with long stinging tentacles. Their venom (poison) can kill in minutes. The stonefish lies hidden under sand. If you step on it, spines on its back inject venom that causes violent pain. The pretty blue-ringed octopus lives in rockpools. Its venom paralyses breathing muscles. Even shells can hurt you. The cone shell, also found in rockpools, has a very painful sting. All these creatures have venom to protect themselves and catch prey.

The venom of the taipan is one of the most deadly in the world. This snake lives in central and northern Australia.

The redback spider (above) likes dark corners. The funnelweb spider (below) attacks by rearing up then stabbing down with fangs full of venom. Both spiders have killed people.

LOOK AGAIN!

Redback spiders have long, needle-like fangs. Funnelwebs have short curved fangs.

The Northern Territory

The Northern Territory is known as 'Outback Australia'. When enough people live there, the Northern Territory will become a self-governing state of Australia.

THE WILD TERRITORY

The territory can be divided into two parts—The Top End and The Red Centre. The Top End has hot weather and lots of rain. The famous Kakadu National Park, north of Katherine, is a wilderness of wetlands, wildlife and wonderful Aboriginal rock paintings. The Red Centre is a place of rolling red sand dunes and amazing rock formations where all living things cope with heat and dry conditions. Almost half of the territory is classified as Aboriginal land and people need special permits to visit these places.

Huge distances are travelled over dirt roads to reach the major cities and ports. Road trains pull one or more trailers loaded with goods.

Cattle are raised for beef on great farms or stations. Cattle workers called jackaroos, round up the cattle using dogs, horses and motor bikes.

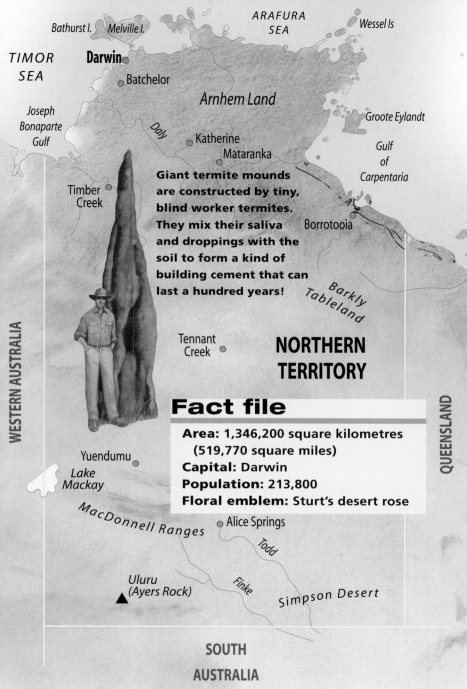

Bathurst I.   Melville I.

ARAFURA SEA

Wessel Is

TIMOR SEA

Darwin

Batchelor

Arnhem Land

Groote Eylandt

Joseph Bonaparte Gulf

Daly

Katherine

Mataranka

Gulf of Carpentaria

Giant termite mounds are constructed by tiny, blind worker termites. They mix their saliva and droppings with the soil to form a kind of building cement that can last a hundred years!

Timber Creek

Borrotooia

Barkly Tableland

Tennant Creek

NORTHERN TERRITORY

WESTERN AUSTRALIA

QUEENSLAND

Fact file

Area: 1,346,200 square kilometres (519,770 square miles)
Capital: Darwin
Population: 213,800
Floral emblem: Sturt's desert rose

Yuendumu

Lake Mackay

MacDonnell Ranges

Alice Springs

Todd

Uluru (Ayers Rock) ▲

Finke

Simpson Desert

SOUTH AUSTRALIA

51

As the land dries, birds crowd into billabongs covered with waterlilies. One third of all the kinds of birds that live in Australia have been seen in Kakadu.

jabiru

brolga

A jabiru stands motionless watching for fish. Across the water the long-legged white brolga digs roots from the mud with its beak. Black and white magpie geese honk overhead.

Kakadu National Park

Wild and beautiful Kakadu has many faces. Near the coast are thick mangrove swamps, shallow lakes (lagoons) and tangled rainforest. Inland are mighty cliffs of red stone.

SUMMER WETLANDS

In the wet season (summer) as much as 5 metres (15 feet) of rain pours down. Waterfalls thunder over the cliffs. Flooded rivers and creeks spill across the coastal plain, turning it into a shining inland sea. Millions of birds share this tropical wetland with frogs, fish, turtles and crocodiles. When the rain stops, the floodwaters shrink into ponds called **billabongs**.

Crocodiles have been around since the time of the dinosaurs, and still look much the same.

Sometimes looking like logs, saltwater crocodiles lie half-submerged in lagoons or sun themselves on the bank. They move with frightening speed to catch food.

Rock on

*Huge rocks stand in the deserts of the Northern Territory. Aboriginal people believe these rocks were shaped by important happenings in the past. They are **sacred** places.*

STORIES IN STONE

Aborigines named this gigantic rock, Uluru. Aboriginal stories tell of a great battle at Uluru. This left marks on the slopes of the rock. Deep potholes are the leg-wounds of a warrior killed in the fighting. The colour of the rock comes from his red body paint and a cave entrance is the mouth of his weeping mother. These stories help explain the landscape.

Uluru

LOOK AGAIN!
What you see of Uluru is only the tip. There is twice as much beneath the sands.

Europeans call these rocks the Devil's Marbles. But to Aboriginal people they are the eggs of the Rainbow Serpent, a spirit-being who formed the land.

Honey ants with bodies swollen with nectar are sweet treats for desert people. The ants hang in tunnels away from the sun.

Both Kata Tjuta and Uluru were once part of the same ancient stony mountain range. The rest of the range was softer rock, and has been worn away.

Kata Tjuta is a collection of high domes and deep valleys, and not a single rock like Uluru.

Living on a station

The huge cattle farms in the outback are called stations. Some are the size of the European country of Belgium. The homestead, or main building, can be like a small village, with an airstrip, workers' quarters, workshop, storerooms, gardens and an orchard.

In an emergency, a Royal Flying Doctor plane can be on the station airstrip in less than two hours to take a seriously ill patient to hospital.

THE LARGEST SCHOOLROOM IN THE WORLD

Outback children do their school work at home. Their classmates are far away on other stations. On school days the children use a radio to speak to the teacher and each other. Watched and helped by a parent, the children do the same subjects as children in town schools, then mail their work to the teacher for marking.

LOOK AGAIN!

There is water under the dry ground. The windmill drives a pump to bring it to the surface.

Towns are few and far apart and the roads are rough and dusty. Mail is picked up and delivered by plane. Some farmers fly their own small planes to town for supplies.

At **mustering** time, **drovers** on horseback are helped by four-wheel-drive vehicles, motorbikes and even helicopters. The dog helps too.

Make your own boomerang

Aboriginal people used boomerangs to hunt. Some were almost straight, some were curved and some were shaped like an 'X'. Very few were designed to come back. They were meant to hit the prey, usually birds. To make your own safe-to-use boomerang you will need a foam food tray, scissors and staples.

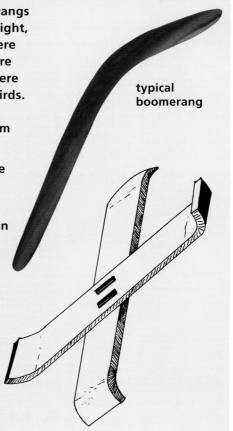

typical boomerang

1. Cut two strips of the same length from the foam food tray.

2. Cross the strips to make an 'X'. Have one strip with curved ends facing down, the other facing up.

3. Staple the strips firmly together.

4. Now your boomerang is ready for action! Find a place where you will not hit anyone and send it whirring into the air.

Key to maps

▨▨▨▨	International border	🗒	Lake, dam or reservoir
⊙ Nairobi	City or Town	**A U S T R A L I A**	Country name
⦿ Sydney	Capital City	*M O U N T A I N S*	Mountain range
————	River	*Susquehanna*	River name

GLOSSARY

ancestor A relative who lived a long time ago.

billabong A waterhole that was once part of a river. It is cut off from the main channel of the river because the river has dried up or because it has changed course.

convict A person who has been found guilty of a crime and who is serving a prison sentence.

flammable Something that is easily set on fire and quick to burn.

fossil The remains of a plant or animal from a long time ago preserved in rock.

germinate When something begins to grow or develop, such as when a plant starts to grow from a seed.

hemisphere One half of a round shape, such as one half of the Earth. The Earth is divided into the northern and southern hemispheres.

immigrant A person who moves to live in a new country or region.

mammal An animal with warm blood and hair or fur, whose young feed on milk from the mother's teats.

marines Soldiers who serve at sea as well as on land.

mate When a male and a female come together to produce young.

monotreme An animal with warm blood and fur that lays eggs. The young feed on milk from the mother.

navigator A person who directs the course of an exploration by sea.

polyp A tiny sea creature that has a soft, tube-shaped body fixed to one place and surrounded by a rock-like skeleton. Coral is made up of thousands of polyps.

sacred Something that is special and respected because it has to do with religion.

INDEX

INDEX

INDEX

COLLECT THE SERIES

INVESTIGATE

AUSTRALIA
Written by Margaret McPhee

PLANES
Illustrated by Spike Wademan

SPIDERS
Illustrated by Frank Knight

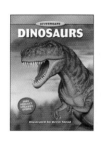

DINOSAURS
Illustrated by Kevin Stead

AFRICA
Written by Judith Simpson

SHARKS
Illustrated by Greg Bridges

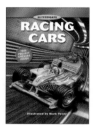

RACING CARS
Illustrated by Mark Vesey

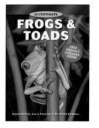

FROGS & TOADS
Illustrated by Garry Fleming & Dr David Kirshner

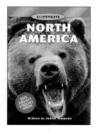

NORTH AMERICA
Written by Judith Simpson

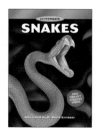

SNAKES
Illustrated by Dr David Kirshner

SPACE
Illustrated by Spike Wademan

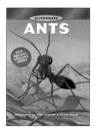

ANTS
Illustrated by Kim Graham & Kevin Stead

SOUTH AMERICA
Written by Margaret McPhee

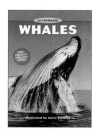

WHALES
Illustrated by Garry Fleming

COMING SOON:
Beetles, Under the Sea, Ships & Boats, Big Cats

Look out for these at your local bookseller

THIS PAGE CAN BE REMOVED